SPIRIT RAPPINGS A FRAUD:

A LECTURE,

DELIVERED DECEMBER 16TH, 1852,

BY JOSEPH F. BERG.

PHILADELPHIA:
WILLIAM S. YOUNG, PRINTER, 50 NORTH SIXTH STREET.
1853.

SPIRIT RAPPINGS A FRAUD.

The question which, by appointment, is before us for discussion, this evening, is a subject which is at present agitating the public mind to an extent which we cannot but regard as unwarranted by sound reason or philosophy. So far as we can ascertain the facts in the history of the phenomena, by a diligent search of the best authenticated authorities, there is no evidence by which the idea of supernatural agency can be satisfactorily established, and so far as regards the so-called spiritual manifestations indicated by rappings, knockings or mysterious noises, we think the burden of the testimony can be so adjusted that every unprejudiced mind will be persuaded that there is nothing more spiritual in these manifestations than may be produced by the ordinary agency of any human spirit controlling the actions of joints and sinews, by the simple power of the will. It is proper that I should notice a single circumstance in justification of my present position in this matter, before entering upon a formal discussion of the facts and evidences which I design to offer in support of the opinion which I have ventured to express in the outset. I have been very courteously invited to satisfy my own mind in relation to the phenomena which appear to settle the controversy in the estimation of some of the believers in the reality of the alleged spiritual agency, by ocular and auricular demonstration; and the proposal has been urged with the plausible argument that, in order to be prepared to speak on this subject fairly, impartially and authoritatively, personal scrutiny is indispensable. I have declined every such overture, not because I shrink from the ordeal under any apprehension of a force of evidence which I might find it difficult to resist or rebut; but for the plain reason that I cannot reconcile this concession on my part with the principles which I hold and which I have publicly expressed. It would not do for me to warn others against entering precincts, and consent to enter them myself. Besides, the whole matter resolves into this simple dilemma. Either the facts and the agency are what they are reported to be, or they are not. Whatever may be the facts, I am perfectly satisfied that the agency is not what is technically called spiritual, and that it is deception on the part of those who are the principals in these transactions, and I must therefore decline being placed in the position of dancing attendance in the antechamber of a clique of rappers, whose joints may be quite as supple as their consciences. On the other hand, if the facts and the agency be as they are reported, then they are nothing more than a revival substantially in another form of arts and devices forbidden in the word of God, upon which no man may wait, and which no man may practise, under penalty of the severest displeasure of Him who is the Father of our spirits. Hence, in either case, I should feel bound by all means to avoid any approach to familiar intercourse with those who, at best, supposing their profession to be literally verified by unexceptionable testimony, are the miserable successors of a fraternity, whose craft bears the impress of Satanic agency, and whom the law of God consigns to infamy in this life, and, unless they repent, to perdition in the life which is to come. Of this we may rest assured: if these professors of demonology can really hold communion with departed spirits, they are spirits whose fellowship is not desirable, and cannot be congenial to any Christian mind or heart, because, inasmuch as all dealing with so called familiar spirits is most expressly and emphatically forbidden in the sacred Scriptures, no good spirit—no spirit sanctified by the Great Spirit of Truth and Holiness would be found lending its sanction to the violation of the precepts of the divine law. If men, therefore, can, in this present life, hold direct communication with departed spirits, they become, when they give utterance to the suggestions of these spirits, the media of evil, depraved and abominable agents, whose whole character and influence are at variance with the truth and government of God. . I am persuaded that in our day, those who desire to maintain the truth on this subject, will find themselves assailed by two different classes of opposition. They will go too far for some, and not far enough for others. They will admit too much for one party, and will reject so much that they will be equally obnoxious to another. There is, however, a medium between the extremes of superstition and fanaticism on the one hand, and on the other, a self-complacent, contemptuous, but none the less ignorant repudiation of truth, which is attested by the highest authority. This authority, which I call the highest, is the Bible.

In discussing the mysterious phenomena which have attracted so much attention at the present time, let us avoid two extremes equally reprehensible. On the one hand, let us beware of a silly credulity which admits any story without examination, however marvellous; and on the other hand, let us guard against that equally stupid propensity utterly to deny the existence of every thing which we cannot explain. I have thought that the most profitable disposition of the subject will be to show that while it is plain, from the most positive representations of the sacred oracles, that communications have been made from the spirit world through the agency of departed spirits, or dæmons, and while, therefore, the abstract possibility of such communications in the ordinary providential administration of the temporal economy, is not to be successfully disputed, no developments which have recently been made can be regarded as falling under this category, but that they are, to a very great extent, the tricks of arrant imposture, or the unexplained phenomena of a magnetic principle, the operation of which is as yet imperfectly understood,—in short, that the intrinsic as well as the extrinsic testimony is altogether adverse to the theory that these are properly spiritual phenomena. If this proposition can be maintained, as I believe, and hope to convince you it can, the grand inference to be drawn from the whole subject will be, that these mysterious sounds and all their correlative details are utterly unworthy of enlightened Christian respect, and that a true regard to reputation for sober intelligence must restrain every well informed person from placing the least dependence upon these alleged revelations from the spirit world. If our time would permit us to enter upon an investigation of the entire testimony of the sacred writings respecting the demoniacal arts practised in the Old Testament age, almost universally prevalent among pagan nations, but always and utterly interdicted to the Hebrews, under the severest penalties, the inquiry would be both relevant to our topic and full of interest, but a less extended range will be amply sufficient to establish all that our present purpose requires. That the practice of consulting spirits obtained in a former age, and that the communications were real and not fanciful, will be apparent from a reference to the following passages:

"Regard not them that have familiar spirits, neither seek after wizards to be defiled by them; I am the Lord your God." (Lev. xix. 31.) "The soul that turneth after such as have familiar spirits, and after wizards to go a whoring after them, I will even set my face against that soul, I will cut him off from among his people." (Lev. xx. 6.) "A man also, or a woman that hath a familiar spirit, or that is a wizard, shall surely be put to death: they shall stone them with stones; their blood shall be upon them." (Lev. xx. 27.) "There shall not be found among you any one, that maketh his son or his daughter to pass through the fire, or that useth divination, or an observer of times, or an enchanter, or a witch, or a charmer, or a consulter with familiar spirits, or a wizard, or a necromancer. For all that do these things are an abomination unto the Lord; and because of these abominations, the Lord thy God doth drive *them*, (i. e. the heathen nations,) out from before thee." (Deut. xviii. 10, 12.) These are passages from the book of the Jewish canon law, and you will observe that in every instance the practice which is interdicted is spoken of not as an illusion, but as a reality. In no single instance is the matter represented as if it were merely a pretence or an imposture; on the contrary, it is throughout treated as a grave matter of fact. "The man or the woman that *hath*," not *that pretendeth to have*, but "that *hath* a familiar spirit shall surely be put to death." If we turn to the historical portion of the Old Testament, we shall find additional testimony, corroborating this position. Of King Manasseh it is said, "He observed times, and used enchantments, and dealt with familiar spirits and wizards: he wrought much wickedness in the sight of the Lord, to provoke him to anger." (2 Kings xxi. 6.) In the narrative of the reign of King Josiah it is recorded—"The workers with familiar spirits, and the wizards, and the images, and the idols, and all the abominations that were spied in the land of Judah, and in Jerusalem, did Josiah put away." (2 Kings xxiii. 24.) But by far the most remarkable incident in the history of these demoniacal communications, is the story of Saul's interview with the witch of Endor,—(1 Sam. xxviii.) and a reference to the chapter will show that this woman was one who had a familiar spirit. When the first suggestion of seeking counsel in his desperation presented itself to the mind of Saul, after he had failed to obtain any response from the Sacred Oracles, in the ordinary and appointed way, he said to his servants, "Seek me a woman that hath a familiar spirit, that I may go to her and inquire of her." Before this account of the King's open apostacy from the worship of God is mentioned, it is expressly stated, "Saul had put away those that had familiar spirits and the wizards out of the land." The whole story of this interview is so worded that on all sound principles of interpretation we are constrained to admit that the historian himself believed that he was narrating a series of incidents which really occurred, and it seems to me utterly derogatory to the character of an inspired history, to suppose that the design was to represent the whole scene as an optical illusion, and that imagination gave a hue of reality to a matter which had no existence in fact. The apparition of Samuel in answer to the call may have been, and doubtless was, permitted in order to inflict the severest possible rebuke upon Saul for his apostacy; for let it be remembered, that under the Old Testament economy, in the Jewish church, the holding of any kind of communication with familiar spirits was regarded as a virtual and open act of apostacy from the faith and fellowship of God's people. This is the only instance on record, and probably the only case which has ever occurred in the whole history of demonolatry, in which the spirit of a just man has ever appeared or given any answer to the summons of a necromancer. In the examination of all these passages, whether of a preceptive or a historical character, the fact will be apparent that in every one of the sixteen instances in which the subject is introduced in the Jewish writings, the matter is spoken of and treated as a *reality*. Whatever actual spiritual influence was at work in this mode of consultation, or divination, was exerted by evil spirits, with the single exception of the case of Samuel, already noticed. This must follow as a necessary consequence from the prohibitory statutes against the practice, for it is manifest that no good spirit would lend its aid to the violation of the divine law. Besides, the thing is spoken of as pertaining to the works of the devil, as a reference to the New Testament authorities will show. The idea seems to be fairly engrafted in the popular theology of the day, that if those dealings with familiar spirits ever were really practised, the period in which they were permitted was antecedent to Christ, or, at all events, that after the death of the Saviour, the works of the devil were so far destroyed that this kind of agency could no longer exist. This theory, however, is not warranted either by the historical, the didactic, or the prophetic portions of the new Testament.

That demoniacal possessions were common in the day of Christ, is manifest from the concurrent testimony of the evangelists—that they were *real* possessions, not epileptic or merely corporeal maladies, is perfectly plain, for the dæmons are represented as speaking, as knowing, and publicly recognising the character of Christ, deprecating his power, and fearing his displeasure; and it would be plainly absurd to predicate any such acts or emotions as pertaining to any other than an intelligent subject. These demoniacal possessions are spoken of as *real*, and we must reject the whole gospel if we reject the testimony which bears upon this point. The subjects of this most terrible calamity were objects of the deepest commiseration, and hence the beneficent power of the Son of God was so frequently exerted in casting out dæmons. Allow me to remark here, as an important fact, which has a very material bearing upon this whole subject, that the word which is invariably employed in these narratives is δαιμων, or δαιμονιον, and that this term, in all the writings of the ancient Greek philosophers and poets, always means *a departed spirit*, i. e., a spirit of a deceased human being. It is used in the same sense by the evangelists and the apostles who wrote in the Greek language. The word *devil* is never used in the New Testament, in the plural number, though it does occur once in that form in the septuagint. In the original, there is a constant distinction maintained between the terms devil and dæmon, and in every instance in which the word "devils" (in the plural form) occurs, the correct rendering would be *dæmons*. I regard this as an exceedingly important distinction, and it throws light upon the agency of departed spirits, which ought not to be overlooked. Abstractly considered, the word dæmon does not necessarily imply a *wicked* spirit; the character of the dæmon is to be ascertained and determined by the employment which engages his powers. Those to which reference is made in the New Testament, were, of course, wicked spirits, and they are called devils in our version, (though improperly) because active in the service of the great Destroyer. With this explanatory observation, let us note a few passages in the apostolic writings, in which this same topic is either casually introduced in the way of historical incident, or noticed in its relation to the doctrines of the Christian system. A remarkable instance is recorded in the Acts of the Apostles, in these words, "And it came to pass, as we went to prayer, a certain damsel possessed with a spirit of divination, met us, which brought her masters much gain by soothsaying: the same followed Paul and us, and cried, saying, These men are the servants of the Most High God, which show unto us the way of salvation. And this she did many days. But Paul being grieved, turned and said to the spirit, I command thee in the name of Jesus Christ to come out of her. And he came out the same hour. And when her masters saw that the hope of their gains was gone, they caught Paul and Silas, and drew them into the market place unto the rulers." Acts xvi. 16, 18. I regard this passage as one of the most important authorities establishing the fact of Satan's agency in the responses of heathen oracles. A spirit of divination is a false spirit of prophecy. Now, we will admit that the absolute, positive knowledge of the future, belongs to God alone, and yet, when we reflect that Satan possesses facilities for observation far superior to any which man has at his command, that his intellect is one of transcendent power, that for nearly 6000 years he has made the physical laws which govern our world his study, that he is the prince of the power of the air, we must admit that his knowledge and power are superhuman, though they are not supernatural. In other words, though he knows more, and can conjecture, and calculate with more than human precision or forecast, and might often suggest signs, and work apparent wonders, as proofs of the authority of a false oracle or a false prophet, Satan cannot work a real miracle. In the case narrated in the book of Acts, the damsel possessed with an evil spirit could foresee events patent to a being in the spirit world *as probable*, and thus she "brought her masters much gain by soothsaying."

If we examine the testimony of the didactic portions of the New Testament, we find that the Apostle Paul regarded the old crime of dealing with familiar spirits as by no means obsolete in his day, for he enumerates witchcraft among the works of the flesh, and you will observe that witchcraft and dealing with familiar spirits are synonymous. He says, "Now the works of the flesh are manifest, which are these, adultery, fornication, uncleanness, lasciviousness, idolatry, *witchcraft*, hatred, variance, emulations," &c., &c. Gal. v. 19, 20. In the prophetic history of the New Testament Church, extending from the age of its primitive establishment, down to the final and glorious consummation of the kingdom of Christ, contained in the Apocalypse, or the revelation of St. John, you will find traces of the same doctrine, and a clear recognition of the existence of Satanic and depraved spiritual agency, even in those portions which relate to the very latest periods of the world's history. In the very last chapter of the Bible, ere the solemn seal is put upon the sacred canon, and men are warned at their peril, neither to add to, nor take from, the words of the prophecy of this book, there is a stern denunciation of this same spiritual wickedness, in the doom which is denounced against "sorcerers," whose place is assigned with them who are *without* the gates of the heavenly city. This, then, may suffice to establish the first part of my proposition, viz., "*That it is plain, from the clearest representations of the sacred oracles, that communications have been made through the agency of departed spirits or dæmons from the spirit world.*"

Next in order, it may be proper to notice briefly a few of the more modern statements which seem to furnish some analogy to the principles and facts substantiated in the sacred scripture. In this department, however, we are met by the most appalling evidences of morbid feeling, running into the wildest excesses of barbarous fanaticism. Two centuries ago, the belief in witchcraft was not only general, but it had degenerated into the most absurd moral epidemic which has ever afflicted humanity. Learning and piety were not a sufficient shield against its deplorable influence. Sir Matthew Hale, one of the greatest jurists that ever adorned the high places of English jurisprudence, sentenced many a poor creature to death, in the conscientious persuasion that he was doing God and his country service, in ridding the earth of the miserable victims of prejudice and calumny, and when the ravings of a disturbed imagination were received in courts of justice as unexceptionable testimony, it is no wonder that a poor lone woman, who lived at a moor side in a miserable hovel, simply because she could find no better home, and who wore a red hood, for no other reason than that she had no other to put on, and lived alone for the best reason in the world, because there was not a living creature in human form that cared a rush whether she was alive or dead, and perchance was seen by some awe-struck traveller, braving the peltings of a merciless storm, in search of brushwood to throw upon the hearth, and soothe her aching limbs, or draw the stiff cold out of her numb fingers, crooked with rheumatism, and because, peradventure, that traveller might have been passing through a gorge, and the poor creature, her red cloak streaming in the wind, was dragging the branch of some decayed tree on the brow of the hill, as a conscientious man, believing in his inmost soul, that he had seen her riding on a broomstick through the wind and rain, far away over his head in the air, he was bound to quit his conscience and tell what he had seen, and the judge and jury were bound to believe him, and the poor woman was relieved of her poverty, her hunger and cold, and her weary nights of racking pain, by the short crisis of suffering on the gallows, or at the fiery stake, and so the land was purged of a witch, and the hovel on the brow of the hill fell into quicker ruin, and the owl built her nest in the chimney, and when at midnight the ominous hoot ot the obscene bird was heard, the peasants said it was the ghost of old Molly the witch, howling in her pain, while a thousand dæmons were chasing her over the moor with burning brands, as the just recompense for having bewitched their cows, and given their hogs the measles. Alas! that it should be so, that a picture such as this should be no fancy sketch, but "an ower true tale" of many a scene of judicial barbarity, perpetrated in an enlightened age, in the name of God and civil justice. One cannot help feeling some relief at the thought, that our Rochester witches did not exercise their toes in making mysterious noises, in merry old England, a century or two ago. They would have paid dearly enough for the rattling of their joints! What a blessed privilege it is to live in a country where a pretty girl may amuse herself and a select party, at a dollar a head, by making the articulations of her limbs discourse mysterious utterances from the spirit world, and not have the fear of Sir Matthew Hale before her eyes.

The virulence of this epidemic of superstitious credulity crops out in the literary monuments of the age. Richard Baxter, a man whose name cannot be mentioned without a feeling of just reverence, wherever profound learning, ardent piety, and unaffected simplicity and meekness are held in esteem, was completely carried away by this morbid enthusiasm. He describes the orgies of the witches in his day, how they used a powder, which immediately transported the spirit out of the body to the trysting spot, where the foul company met and danced with Satan, who appeared in the form of a he-goat, and how they did many naughty things, which this deponent sayeth not; and how when chanticleer sounded his matin horn, and the ghosts snuffed the morning air, swift as the wind, the wicked witches straddled their broom sticks and hied home to have the porridge ready by the time the good man was awake and hungry for his breakfast. Then the good Baxter will tell you of other phenomena, which were described to him by unexceptionable witnesses, and through the exaggerations of which, you may trace the features of some mesmeric pranks, as the real foundation and rationale of the whole affair. Then, there is a chapter in the early history of our own country, and it is a sad chapter, but it cannot be blotted out, and a wise Providence has, doubtless, permitted its enaction on a comparatively small scale in mercy, in order forever to bar the door against its re-enactment in a more extensive form. I allude to the history of the Salem witchcraft. Our Puritan fathers inherited this morbid faith in the power of witches from the age, and they brought it with them and enshrined it, unhappily for the victims, in the altars which they had reared to the worship of the God whose service is freedom, and whom they adored as the only Lord of the conscience. No man who understands, or who has ever tried to investigate the anatomy of character, will doubt for a moment that Cotton Mather was an earnest, devout, and godly man. That he was, moreover, a ripe scholar and a man of uncommonly strong natural powers of mind, by no means deficient in discernment, will be plain to every one, who will be at the pains to read his Magnalia; but all these eminent qualities did not protect him from the virus of the witch-mania—he was inoculated, and the plague subdued him, and made his great powers the sincere ministers of a wretched fanaticism. Among those who were accused of witchcraft, and who were condemned and executed for the same, was one George Burroughs, a minister of the gospel—one who had for ten years maintained an unimpeachable character, and it may not be uninteresting to glance at the testimony, upon the strength of which he was convicted, as Mather himself records it in his Magnalia.

"Can we do better than to listen for a short time to the account of this thing from the venerable Magnalia.* 'Glad should I have been, if I had never known the name of this man, this George Burroughs—or never had this occasion to mention so much as the first letters of his name.

"1. This G. B. was indicted for witchcraft. He was accused by eight of the confessing witches, as being the head actor at some of their hellish rendezvous, and who had the promise of being a king in Satan's kingdom now going to be erected: he was accused by nine persons for extraordinary lifting and such feats of strength as could not be done without a diabolical assistance; and for other such things he was accused, until about thirty testimonies were brought in against him; nor were these judged the half of what might have been considered for his conviction; however, they were enough to fix the character of a witch upon him, according to the rules of reasoning by the judicious Gaule in that case directed.

"2. The court being sensible that the testimonies of the parties bewitched used to have room among the suspicious or presumptuous, brought in against one indicted for witchcraft, there were now heard the testimonies

* Wonders of I. W. pp. 33 to 39.

of several persons who were most notoriously bewitched, and every day tortured by invisible hands, and these now all charged the spectres of G. B. to have a share in their torments. At the examination of this G. B. the bewitched people were grievously harassed with preternatural mischiefs, which could not possibly [?] be dissembled; and they still ascribed unto the endeavours of G. B. to kill them. And now upon his trial one of the bewitched persons testified, that in her agonies a little black-haired man came to her, saying his name was B., and bidding her set her hand to a book which he showed unto her, and bragging that he was a conjurer above the ordinary rank of witches; that he often persecuted her with the offer of that book, saying she should be well and need fear nobody, if she would but sign it, but he inflicted cruel pains and hurts upon her because of her denying to do so. The testimonies of the other sufferers concurred with these; and it was remarkable that whereas biting was one of the ways which the witches used for the vexing of sufferers, when they cried out of G. B. biting them, the print of his teeth would be seen on the flesh of the complainers, and just such a set of teeth as G. B.'s would then appear on them, which could be distinguished from those of some other men's.

"Others of them testified, that in their torments G. B. tempted them to go into a sacrament, unto which they perceived him with a sound of a trumpet summoning other witches, who quickly after the sound would come from all quarters unto the rendezvous. One of them falling into a kind of trance, affirms afterward that G. B. had carried her into a very high mountain, where he showed her mighty and glorious kingdoms, and said he would give them all to her if she would write in his book, but she told him they were none of his to give, and refused the motion, enduring much misery for the refusal.

"It cost the court a wonderful deal of trouble to hear the testimonies of the sufferers. For when they were going to give in their depositions, they would for a long time be taken with fits, that made them incapable of saying any thing. The Chief Judge asked the prisoner who he thought hindered these witnesses from giving their testimonies, and he answered he supposed it was the Devil. That honourable person then replied, 'How comes the Devil to be so loath to hear any testimony borne against you?' which cast him into very great confusion.

"3. It hath been a frequent thing for the bewitched people to be entertained with apparitions of ghosts of murdered people, at the same time that the spectres of the witches troubled them. These ghosts do always affright the beholders, more than all the other spectral representations; and when they exhibit themselves, they cry out of being murdered by the witchcrafts or other violences of the persons who are then in spectre present. It is further considered that once or twice these apparitions have been seen by others, at the very same time they have shown themselves to be bewitched, and seldom have there been these apparitions, but when something unusual and suspected hath attended the death of the party thus appearing. Some that have been accused by these apparitions, accosting the bewitched people, who had never heard a word of any such persons ever being in the world, have upon a fair examination, freely and fully confessed the murder of those very persons, although these also did not know how the apparitions had complained of them. Accordingly, several of the bewitched had given in their testimony, that they had been troubled with the apparitions of two women, who said they were G. B.'s two wives, and that he had been the death of them, and that the magistrates must be told of it, before whom, if G. B. upon his trial denied it, they did not know but that they should appear again in the court. Now G. B. had been infamous for the barbarous usage of his two successive wives, all the country over. Moreover it was testified, the spectre of G. B. threatening the sufferers told them he had killed (beside others) Mrs. Lawson and her daughter Ann. And it was noted that these were the virtuous wife and daughter of one at whom this G. B. might have a prejudice for being serviceable at Salem village, from whence himself had in ill terms removed some years before; and that when they died, which was long since, there were some odd circumstances about them, which made some of the attendants there suspect witchcraft, though none imagined from what quarter it should come.

"Well, G. B. being now upon his trial, one of the bewitched persons was cast into horror at the ghosts of B.'s two deceased wives then appearing before him, and crying for vengeance against him. Hereupon several of the bewitched persons were successively called in, who all not knowing what the former had seen and said, concurred in their horror of the apparition, which they affirmed that he had before him. But he, though much appalled, utterly denied that he discerned any thing of it, nor was it any part of his conviction.

"4. Judicious writers have assigned it a great place in the conviction of witches, when persons are impeached by other notorious witches to be as ill as themselves, especially if the persons have been much noted for neglecting the worship of God. Now as there might have been testimonies enough of G. B.'s antipathy to prayer, and the other ordinances of God, though by his profession singularly obliged thereunto; so there now came in against the prisoner, the testimonies of several persons, who confessed their own having been horrible witches, and ever since their confessions had been themselves terribly tortured by the devils and other witches, even like the other sufferers, and therein undergone the pains of many deaths for their confessions.

"These now testified that G. B. had been at witch meetings with them, and that he was the person who had seduced and compelled them into the snares of witchcraft, that he promised them fine clothes for doing it; that he brought them poppets and thorns to stick into those poppets, for the afflicting of other people; and that he exhorted them with the rest of the crew to bewitch all Salem village; but be sure to do it gradually, if they would prevail in what they did.

"When the Lancashire witches were condemned, I do not remember that there was any considerable further evidence than that of the bewitched, and than that of some that had confessed; we see so much already against G. B. But this being indeed not enough, there were other things to render what had already been produced credible.

"5. A famous divine recites this among the convictions of a witch, the testimony of the party bewitched whether pining or dying, together with the joint oaths of sufficient persons that have seen certain prodigious pranks or feats wrought by the party accused. Now God [?] had been pleased so to leave G. B., that he had insnared himself by several instances which he had formerly given, of a preternatural strength, and which were now producèd against him. He was a very puny man, yet he had often done things beyond the strength of a giant. A gun of about seven feet barrel, and so heavy that strong men could not steadily hold it out, with both hands: there were several testimonies given in by persons of credit and honour, that he made nothing of taking up such a gun behind the lock with but one hand, and holding it out like a pistol at arm's length. G. B. in his vindication was so foolish as to say that an Indian was there and held it out, at the same time; whereas none of the spectators saw any such Indian; but they supposed the black man (as the witches call the Devil, and they generally say he resembles an Indian) might give him that assistance. There was evidence brought in that he made nothing of taking up whole barrels filled with molasses or cider in very disadvantageous postures, and carrying them off, through the most difficult places, out of a canoe to the shore.

"Yea, there were two testimonies that G. B., with only putting the forefinger of his right hand into the muzzle of an heavy gun, a fowling-piece, of about six or seven feet barrel, lifted the gun, and held it out at arm's end; a gun which the deponents, though strong men, could not with both hands lift up, and hold out at the butt end, as is usual. Indeed one of the witnesses was over-persuaded by some persons to be out of the way upon G. B.'s trial, but he came afterward with sorrow for his withdrawing, and gave in his testimony. Nor were either of these witnesses made use of as evidence in the trial.

"6. Then came in several testimonies relating to the domestic affairs of G. B., which had a very hard aspect upon him; and not only proved him a very ill man, but also confirmed the belief of the character which had already been fastened upon him. 'Twas testified that keeping his two successive wives in a strange kind of slavery, he would, when he came home from abroad, pretend to tell the talk which any had with them: that he has brought them to the point of death by his harsh dealings with his wives, and then made the people about him promise that in case death should happen they would say nothing of it; that he used all means to make his wives write, sign, seal, and swear, a covenant never to reveal any of his secrets; that his wives had privately complained unto the neighbours about frightly apparitions of evil spirits, with which their house was sometimes infested; and that many such things had been whispered among the neighbourhood. There were also some other testimonies relating to the death of people, whereby the consciences of an impartial jury were convinced that G. B. had bewitched the persons mentioned in the complaints. But I am forced to omit several such passages in this as well as all the succeeding trials, because the scribes who took notice of them have not supplied me.

"7. One Mr. Ruck, brother-in-law to this G. B., testified that G. B. and he himself, and his sister, who was G. B.'s wife, going out for two or three miles to gather strawberries, Ruck with his sister, the wife of G. B. rode home very softly, with G. B. on foot in their company; G. B. stepped aside a little into the bushes, whereupon they halted and halloed for him; he not answering, they went away homewards, with a quickened pace, without any expectation of seeing him in a considerable while; and yet when they were got near home, to their astonishment they found him on foot with them, having a basket of strawberries. G. B. immediately fell to chiding his wife on account of what she had been speaking to her brother of him on the road: which, when they wondered at, he said he knew their thoughts. Ruck being startled at that, made some reply, intimating that the Devil did not know so far: but G. B. answered, my God makes known your thoughts unto me. The prisoner now at the bar had nothing to answer to what was thus witnessed against him that was worth considering: only he said Ruck and his wife left a man with him when they left him; which Ruck now affirmed to be false, and when the court asked G. B. what the man's name was, his countenance was much altered, nor could he say who it was. But the court began to think that he then stepped aside, only that by the assistance of the black man he might put on his invisibility, and in that fascinating mist gratify his own jealous humour to hear what they said of him—which trick of rendering themselves invisible our witches do in their confessions pretend that they sometimes are masters of; and it is the more credible, because there is demonstration that they often render many other things utterly invisible.

"8. Faltering, faulty, unconstant, and contrary answers, upon judicial and deliberate examination, are counted some unlucky symptoms of guilt in all crimes, especially in witchcrafts. Now there never was a prisoner more eminent for these than G. B. both at his examination and on his trial. His tergiversations, contradictions and falsehoods, were very sensible; he had little to say, but that he had heard some things that he could not prove reflecting upon the character of some of the witnesses; only he gave in a paper to the jury, wherein, although he had many times before granted not only that there are witches, but also that the present sufferings of the country are the effects of horrible witchcrafts, yet he now goes to evince it that there neither are, nor ever were witches, that having made a compact with the devil, can send a devil to torment other people at a distance. This paper was transcribed out of Ady—which the court presently knew as soon as they heard it. But he said he had taken none of it out of any book; for which his evasion afterwards was, that a gentleman gave him the discourse in a manuscript, from whence he had transcribed it.

"9. The jury brought him in guilty; but when he came to die, he utterly denied the fact whereof he had been thus convicted."

This may serve as a specimen. Poor George Burroughs! Thine was a hard lot; and yet the sacrifice was not in vain. God never suffers an innocent man to be put to death, without making that very injustice ultimately accomplish a righteous purpose. History has been defined as "philosophy teaching by example," and a few such examples may serve as the tower that shoots up from the summit of a rugged rock in the midst of the stormy ocean, and by the light of its watch fire warns the mariner of the reef upon which many a noble vessel has been wrecked. You will see, in the narrative of this testimony, some probability that Burroughs was a subject out of which some of the modern professors of mesmeric science might have made a profitable medium. This animal magnetism, or sympathetic power, is a strange thing. On a former occasion I stated one experiment, which I have witnessed, and I made allusion to another, which, although differing in its details, established no new principle, whilst confirming the same law. I have seen a man, and when I name him every person in this house will know him, none other than John Smith, whilst in a mesmeric state, though by no means naturally endowed with unusual muscular strength, lift a chair from the floor with all ease, in spite of the efforts of four able-bodied men to keep it in its place, and scatter the four persons whose combined strength offered an ineffectual resistance, giving them some trouble to keep their feet; and it is not unlikely that this poor Burroughs possessed a similar power, and could lift a gun in the manner described, though in his normal, ordinary condition, unable to perform any such feat. I can testify, however, that John Smith does not come up to the standard of qualifications required in order to convict him of witchcraft.

Another case, which presents a closer analogy to the knockings of which we have heard so much, is contained in a narrative drawn up and published by no less a man than the venerable John Wesley. I will not stop to prove that the character of the narrator is a sufficient guarantee for sincerity. He believed what he stated to be true, whether the facts were as he presented them or not. If you will not be frightened out of your propriety, we will give you the story in John Wesley's own words.

"When I was very young, I heard several letters read, wrote to my elder brother by my father, giving an account of strange disturbances, which were in his house at Epworth, Lincolnshire.

"When I went down thither, in the year 1720, I carefully inquired into the particulars. I spoke to each of the persons who were then in the house, and took down what each could testify, of his or her own knowledge, the sum of which was this:—

"On December 2nd, 1716, while Robert Brown, my father's servant, was sitting with one of the maids, a little before ten at night, in the dining room, which opened into the garden, they both heard one knocking at the door. Quickly it knocked again, and groaned. 'It is Mr. Turpine,' said Robert; 'he has the stone, and used to groan so.' He opened the door again twice or thrice, the knocking being twice or thrice repeated; but still seeing nothing, and being a little startled, they rose and went up to bed. When Robert came to the top of the garret stairs, he saw a hand-mill, which was at a little distance, whirled about very swiftly. The next day, he and the maid related these things to the other maid, who laughed heartily, and said: 'What a couple of fools you are! I defy any thing to fright me.' After churning in the evening, she put the butter in the tray, and had no sooner carried it into the dairy, than she heard a knocking on the shelf where several puncheons of milk stood, first above the shelf, then below. She took the candle, and searched both above and below; but being able to find nothing, threw down butter, tray and all, and ran away for life. The next evening, between five and six o'clock, my sister Molly, then about twenty years of age, sitting in the dining-room reading, heard, as if it were, the door that led into the hall, open, and a person walking in, that seemed to have on a silk night-gown, rustling and trailing along. It seemed to walk round her, then to the door, then round again; but she could see nothing. She thought, 'It signifies nothing to run away; for, whatever it is, it can run faster than I.' So she rose, put her book under her arm, and walked slowly away. After supper, she was sitting with my sister Sukey, (about a year older than her,) in one of the chambers, and telling her what had happened. She made quite light of it, telling her, 'I wonder you are so easily frightened; I would fain see what would fright me.' Presently a knocking began under the table. She took the candle and looked, but could find nothing. Then the iron casement began to clatter, and the lid of a warming-pan. Next the latch of the door moved up and down without ceasing. She started up, leaped into the bed without undressing, pulled the bed-clothes over her head, and never ventured to look up till next morning. A night or two after, my sister Hetty, a year younger than my sister Molly, was waiting, as usual, between nine and ten, to take away my father's candle, when she heard one coming down the garret stairs, walking slowly by her, then going down the best stairs, then up the back stairs, and up the garret stairs; at every step it seemed the house shook from top to bottom. Just then my father knocked. She went in, took his candle, and got to bed as soon as possible. In the morning she told this to my eldest sister, who told her, 'You know I believe none of these things; pray let me take away the candle to-night, and I will find out the trick.' She accordingly took my sister Hetty's place, and had no sooner taken away the candle than she heard a noise below. She hastened down stairs to the hall, where the noise was; but it was then in the kitchen. She run into the kitchen, where it was drumming on the inside of the screen. When she went round, it was drumming on the outside; and so always on the side opposite to her. Then she heard a knocking at the back kitchen door. She ran to it, unlocked it softly, and when the knocking was repeated, suddenly opened it; but nothing was to be seen. As soon as she had shut it, the knocking began again. She opened it again, but could see nothing. When she went to shut the door, it was violently thrust against her; she let it fly open, but nothing appeared. She went again to shut it, and it was again thrust against her; but she set her knee and her shoulder to the door, forced it to, and turned the key. Then the knocking began again; but she let it go on, and went up to bed. However, from that time she was thoroughly convinced that there was no imposture in the affair.

"The next morning, my sister telling my mother what had happened, she said, 'If I hear any thing myself, I shall know how to judge.' Soon after, she begged her to come into the nursery. She did, and heard in the corner of the room, as it were, the violent rocking of a cradle; but no cradle had been there for some years. She was convinced it was preternatural, and earnestly prayed it might not disturb her in her own chamber at the hours of retirement; and it never did. She now thought it was proper to tell my father. But he was extremely angry, and said: 'Sukey, I am ashamed of you; these boys and girls frighten one another; but you are a woman of sense, and should know better. Let me hear of it no more.'

"At six in the evening he had family prayers, as usual. When he began the prayer for the king, a knocking began all around the room; and a thundering knock attended the amen. The same was heard, from this time, every morning and evening, while the prayer for the king was repeated.

"Being informed that Mr. Hoole, the vicar of Haxley, (an eminently pious and sensible man,) could give me some further information, I walked over to him. He said, 'Robert Brown came over to me, and told me your father desired my company. When I came, he gave me an account of all that had happened; particularly the knocking during family prayer. But that evening (to my great satisfaction) we had no knocking at all. But between nine and ten a servant came in, and said, "Old Jeffrey is coming, (that was the name of one that died in the house,) for I hear the signal." This, they informed me, was heard every night about a quarter before ten. It was toward the top of the house, on the outside, at the north-east corner, resembling the loud creaking of a saw; or rather that of a wind-mill, when the body of it is turned about, in order to shift the sails to the wind. We then heard a knocking over our heads; and Mr. Wesley, catching up a candle, said, "Come, sir, now you shall hear for yourself." We went up stairs; he with much hope, and I, to say the truth, with much fear. When we came into the nursery, it was knocking in the next room; when we were there it was knocking in the nursery. And there it continued to knock, though we came in, particularly at the head of the bed, (which was of wood,) in which Miss Hetty and two of her younger sisters lay. Mr. Wesley, observing that they were much affected, though asleep, sweating and trembling exceedingly, was very angry; and, pulling out a pistol, was going to fire at the place from whence the sound came. But I catched him by the arm, and said, "Sir, you are convinced this is something preternatural. If so, you cannot hurt it; but you give it power to hurt you." He then went close to the place, and said sternly, "Thou deaf and dumb devil, why dost thou fright these children, that cannot answer for themselves? Come to me in my study, that am a man." Instantly it knocked his knock, (the particular knock which he always used at the gate,) as if it would shiver the board in pieces, and we heard nothing more that night.' Till this time my father had never heard the least disturbances in his study. But the next evening, as he attempted to go into his study, (of which none had any key but himself,) when he opened the door, it was thrust back with such violence as had like to have thrown him down. However, he thrust the door open, and went in. Presently there was knocking, first on one side, then on the other; and, after a time, in the next room, wherein my sister Nancy was. He went into that room, and (the noise continuing) adjured it to speak; but in vain. He then said, 'These spirits love darkness; put out the candle, and perhaps it will speak.' She did so, and he repeated his adjuration; but still there was only knocking, and no articulate sound. Upon this he said, 'Nancy, two Christians are an overmatch for the devil. Go all of you down stairs; it may be, when I am alone, he will have courage to speak.' When she was gone, a thought came in, and he said, 'If thou art the spirit of my son Samuel, I pray knock three knocks, and no more.' Immediately all was silence; and there was no more knocking at all that night. I asked my sister Nancy (then about fifteen years old) whether she was not afraid when my father used that adjuration? She answered she was sadly afraid it would speak when she put out the candle; but she was not at all afraid in the daytime, when it walked after her as she swept the chambers, as it constantly did, and seemed to sweep after her; only she thought he might have done it for her, and saved her the trouble. By this time, all my sisters were so accustomed to these noises, that they gave them little disturbance. A gentle tapping at their bed-head usually began between nine and ten at night. They then commonly said to each other, 'Jeffrey is coming; it is time to go to sleep.' And if they heard a noise in the day, and said to my youngest sister, 'Hark, Kezzy, Jeffrey is knocking above,' she would run up stairs, and pursue it from room to room, saying she desired no better diversion.

"'A few nights after, my father and mother were just gone to bed, and the candle was not taken away, when they heard three blows, and a second, and a third, three, as it were with a large oaken staff, struck upon a chest which stood by the bed-side. My father immediately arose, put on his night-gown, and hearing great noises below, took the candle and went down; my mother walked by his side. As they went down the broad stairs, they heard as if a vessel full of silver was poured upon my mother's breast, and ran jingling down to her feet.—Quickly after there was a sound, as if a large iron ball was thrown among many bottles under the stairs; but nothing was hurt. Soon after, our large mastiff dog came and ran to shelter himself between them. While the disturbances continued, he used to bark and leap, and snap on one side and the other, and that frequently before any person in the room heard any noise at all. But after two or three days he used to tremble, and creep away before the noise began. And by this, the family knew it was at hand; nor did the observation ever fail. A little before my father and mother came into the hall, it seemed as if a very large coal was violently thrown upon the floor, and dashed all in pieces; but nothing was seen. My father then cried out, 'Sukey, do you not hear? All the pewter is thrown about the kitchen.' But when they looked, all the pewter stood in its place. There then was a loud knocking at the back door. My father opened it, but saw nothing. It was then at the fore door. He opened that, but it was still lost labour. After opening first the one, then the other, several times, he turned and went up to bed. But the noises were so violent all over the house, that they could not sleep till four in the morning.

"'Several gentlemen and clergymen now earnestly advised my father to quit the house. But he constantly answered, 'No; let the devil flee from me; I will never flee from the devil.' But he wrote to my eldest brother, at London, to come down. He was preparing so to do, when another letter came, informing him the disturbances were over, after they had continued, the latter part of the time, day and night, from the second of December to the end of January.'"

This curious history, for the insertion of which some have been disposed to chide us, because it seems to adduce authority against our theory, admits of some criticism, without any disparagement of the veracity of John Wesley. One circumstance which weighs against the ghostly origin of these phenomena is presented in the conduct of the girl, who seemed to relish the fun of chasing the ghost from room to room. We suggest that she was a *medium*, and knew more about the origin of these mysterious noises than she chose to divulge. In this respect, she was not unlike some other children who have vexed the credulity of their parents. Young ladies are not usually so fond of ghosts as to run after them, and Kezzy would probably not have been an exception had she not been herself the *spook*, making these rappings by a trick of her own; in this way she might very easily have gone from room to room, and the only blunder in the narrative would in that case be, the not uncommon one of putting the cart before the horse. The noises followed her instead of her following the noises. There were *knockings* in this case, you will observe. The question has been proposed to me, How can a spirit produce knockings? How can a spirit, in other words, act upon matter? The objection is intended to weigh against the possibility of a series of such phenomena being produced by a spiritual agent, but we must treat this subject in candour, and I think I can very soon convince you, that if we had no stronger argument to offer, we should soon be left in the vocative. A spirit can act upon matter, and every person in this assembly is a living witness of the truth. If I rap upon this desk, you hear a sound. What produces it? Why, you will say, the violent contact of your knuckles with the hard board. True enough, so far as it goes, but was it my hand that rapped, or was it my spirit that used this hand in the exercise of its will? I think the latter is the more philosophical explanation of the two. What is the eye but the window out of which the soul looks? It is not the eye that sees, it is the spirit that sees through the eye, as its organ of vision, whilst it is in the body, and so of every other faculty. This, however, we shall be told again, is not exactly the question. We will therefore change its form. Can a disembodied spirit act upon matter? I answer again, most undoubtedly. Who made this earth out of things which do not appear? Who created the heavens and stretched them out as a curtain? Who spread forth the earth and that which cometh out of it? Who gave breath unto the people upon it, and spirit to them that walk thereon? It was God. And is not God a spirit? Verily. The sea is his, and he made it, and his hands formed the dry land. Surely a spirit can act upon matter. A spirit is a living substance, not a dead shadow. A mighty angel, at the resurrection of our Lord, came and rolled away the stone from the mouth of the sepulchre and sat upon it. And what are angels? Are they not all ministering *spirits?* This objection, therefore, will not stand the test of enlightened reason. A spirit can act upon matter. How then about the Rochester knockings, and the Arch Street rappings? Are they spiritual manifestations? Yes, precisely in principle, as this is a spiritual manifestation, when I bring my knuckles down upon this board! But, this is a hard saying. Perhaps so, but I believe it is the truth, and I think I can prove it. My opinion is based upon the following evidence, which comes with the sanction of responsible names, men of eminence in their profession, and it is unexceptionable, and to my mind, conclusive. The following is the report of a committee, consisting of Drs. Flint, Lee and Coventry, who investigated this *striking* humbug on the simplest principle of nature, and succeeded in exposing as arrant a piece of imposture as ever tormented human credulity.

[From the Buffalo Medical Journal.]

All our readers have heard of the *Rochester knockings* that have occasioned not a little stir in different parts of the country during the past two or three years. The *knockings* were first manifested in a family of the name of Fox, then residing in a small town in the western part of this State, and the removal of this family, shortly afterward, to Rochester, whence have emanated many of the marvellous stories connected with the subject, has secured for that city the honour of forming the adjective in the title by which they are commonly mentioned. The *knockings*, however, have not been confined to Rochester, but have been heard in some other places. They accompany members of the Fox family in their peregrinations, of course, but we understand that other persons than those belonging to this family have assumed to be *media* for similar supernatural manifestations.

Being regarded by the credulous and superstitious as phenomena produced by the agency of departed spirits, indicating their presence, and furnishing a means of communication with them, it is not singular that, however ridiculous the subject may seem to persons of well balanced minds, to those of a different mental cast, it assumes a different aspect, and becomes invested with great interest and importance. In every community persons are to be found who are fond of indulging and cultivating a love for what is marvellous, and who are ready to believe that a supernatural agency is involved in whatever transcends their comprehension. Such tendencies are by no means found in connexion exclusively with low intellectual powers, and small attainments. On the contrary, it is not unfrequently the case that persons of education, of reflection, and even of superior mental endowments in some respects, are led astray by what appeals strongly to the mental qualities underlying an unfortunate excess of credulity. The chicaneries of Mesmerism, the faith inspired by revelations like those of Davis, etc., sufficiently attest the truth of the remark just made. We might also quote, as illustrations, the transient success of homœopathy, and other kindred medical delusions. The annals of every age furnish abundance of examples showing the absurd extravagances into which men may be led who allow unrestrained scope to the imaginative and superstitious elements of the mental constitution; showing, also, the astonishing extent to which cunning impostors are able to take advantage of these elements of human character. Based, as are the various delusions, impositions, and humbugs that prove successful, upon qualities of mind which it is not to be expected will soon cease to be predominant in certain individuals, albeit science and knowledge are progressively advancing, and despite the accumulated lesson of experience, we are not to suppose that the future, more than the past and present, will be devoid of instances exemplifying human weakness and folly like that to which reference has been made. But to return to the *Rochester knockings*. We have not taken pains to ascertain how extensively belief in their supernatural character has prevailed. Many of our readers are probably better informed on this point than ourselves, as our pursuits do not permit us to keep up with the times in matters of this kind. That many well meaning persons have been beguiled and carried away with this subject, we know, and that not a little time, money, thought, and feeling, have been expended in the efforts to hold communion, by *rappings*, with the inhabitants of the spirit world, is a fact but too apparent to any one who looks into newspapers. The imposition, unfortunately, is not to be considered merely a successful but harmless experiment on the exhaustless fund of human credulity. Among other serious consequences, we have been told that several cases of insanity have originated in the mental excitement occasioned by fancied intercourse with the spirits of departed friends.

The imposition, which had already escaped detection for several years, would still find plenty of dupes, if the *mysterious sounds* were to continue unaccounted for. The absurdity of the professed spirituality of the knockings can undoubtedly be fully proved in a variety of modes, but the only effectual preventive of the farther progress of the humbug is to determine satisfactorily their nature and source. To do this is to strike at the root of the delusion by rendering it as ridiculous as the explanation is simple. We are not aware that the curious and (in other than a literal sense) striking phenomena have been, as yet, accounted for. To what extent they have been made the subject of investigation by physicians we cannot say. As we are prepared to unravel the mystery, we trust our readers will not think the subject unworthy the space which we propose to devote to it, more especially as the sounds possess interest in a physiological point of view, apart from the remarkable imposition to which they have been made subservient.

Two members of the celebrated family of *Rochester knockers* recently made their debut in this city, accompanied by the noisy spirits, and commenced operations, drawing crowds of visiters at a dollar a head, many of whom were impressed with the wonderful revelations interpreted from the *raps*, and several intelligent persons became converts to the doctrine of the spiritual origin of the sounds. From motives of curiosity we were

2

led, with our colleagues, to pay them a visit, and, we must confess, we were surprised and puzzled by the loudness of the sounds, the apparent evidences of non-instrumentality on the part of the females, and the different directions from which they seemed to emanate. Close observation, however, of the countenances and deportment of the two females, led to the conviction that the production of the sounds involved a voluntary effort by the younger sister of the two—a girl about seventeen years of age, the elder sister (who is said to be a widow) being about thirty-five. The latter was apparently the *managing partner,* conducting the spiritual communications, while the former, it was clear, was the performer, i. e. the one that produced the knockings. Assuming the above as a point of departure, by the process of reasoning given below, the diagnosis was, that the sounds must necessarily be articular. This conclusion and the process by which it was arrived at, were stated to a number of persons directly after the visit. The question then was, how such sounds could come from joints. The snapping of the phalangal joints of one hand by the lateral motions made with the other hand, is familiar to every one. Some persons have the power to produce the same snapping by means of the muscles inserted into the phalangal bones, without any aid from the other hand. Dislocated bones return to their place with an audible snap, as all surgeons know. A patient once consulted us for a loud noise in his joint produced by walking. Almost every one has occasionally, by an accidental oblique movement of the lower extremities, caused a loud report in the knee joint. These facts suggested themselves, but works on physiology, anatomy, and dislocations, were consulted, in vain, for any account of loud noises like the *Rochester knockings* originating in the articulations. While pursuing these inquiries, which had been unexpectedly provoked, we chanced to meet with a person who said that his wife could produce similar sounds. He did not then know in what way they were produced; his wife had, in jest, kept him in ignorance on this point. At our request he immediately went home to ascertain, and returned with the information that the noise came from the knee joint, and that we were at liberty to satisfy ourselves with respect to this fact, and also of the mode in which they were produced. Accordingly, at first alone, and afterward accompanied by Drs. Lee and Coventry (in concert with whom the prior investigations were conducted), we visited the lady referred to, and on the following day the subjoined exposition was communicated for one of the daily papers of the city.*

To the Editor of the Commercial Advertiser:

Curiosity having led us to visit the room at the Phelps House in which two females from Rochester (Mrs. Fish and Miss Fox,) profess to exhibit *striking* manifestations of the spiritual world, by means of which communion may be held with deceased friends, &c., and having arrived at a physiological explanation of the phenomena, the correctness of which has

* In transferring that communication to our columns, we have corrected an error in the account of the displacement of the joint which produces the sounds. The exposition was drawn up hastily, and published at once, in order to check as promptly as practicable the farther progress of the imposition, and the mechanism was not so fully ascertained, as it has been by subsequent examinations. We will thank editors of medical journals who may notice this matter to copy the anatomical explanation from this article, and not from the newspaper, and to make the correction referred to, should they have already quoted the first statement.

been demonstrated in an instance that has since fallen under observation, we have felt that a public statement is called for, which may perhaps serve to prevent further waste of time, money, and credulity (to say nothing of sentiment and philosophy,) in connexion with this so long successful imposition.

The explanation is reached almost by a logical necessity, on the application of a method of reasoning much resorted to in the diagnosis of diseases, viz.: *reasoning by way of exclusion.* It was reached by this method prior to the demonstration which has subsequently occurred.

It is to be assumed, first, that the manifestations are not to be regarded as spiritual, provided they can be physically, or physiologically accounted for. Immaterial agencies are not to be invoked until material agencies fail. We are thus to *exclude* spiritual causation in this stage of the investigation.

Next, it is taken for granted that the *rappings* are not produced by artificial contrivances about the persons of the females, which may be concealed by the dress. This hypothesis is excluded, because it is understood that the females have been repeatedly and carefully examined by lady committees.

It is obvious that the rappings are not caused by machinery attached to tables, doors, etc., for they are heard in different rooms, and different parts of the same room, in which the females are present, but always *near* the spot where the females are stationed. This mechanical hypothesis is then to be *excluded.*

So much for *negative* evidence, and now for what *positively* relates to the subject.

On carefully observing the countenances of the two females, it was evident that the sounds were due to the agency of the younger sister, and that they involved an effort of the will. She evidently attempted to conceal any indications of voluntary effort, but in this she did not succeed:—a voluntary effort was manifest, and it was plain that it could not be continued very long without fatigue.

Assuming, then, this positive fact, the inquiry arises, how can the will be exerted to produce sounds (rappings) without obvious movements of the body? The voluntary muscles are the only organs (save those which belong to the mind itself) over which volition can exert any direct control. But the contractions of the muscles do not, in the muscles themselves, occasion obvious sounds. The muscles, therefore, to develope audible vibrations, must act upon parts with which they are connected. Now, it was sufficiently clear that the rappings were not *vocal* sounds: these could not be produced without movements of the respiratory muscles, which would at once lead to detection. Hence, *excluding* vocal sounds, the only *possible* source of the noise in question, produced, as we have seen they must be, by voluntary muscular contractions, is one or more of the movable articulations of the skeleton. From the anatomical connexions of the voluntary muscles, this explanation remains as the only alternative.

By an analysis prosecuted in this manner, we arrive at the conviction that the *rappings,* assuming that they are not spiritual, are produced by the action of the will, through voluntary muscles upon the joints.

Various facts may be cited to show that the motion of joints, under certain circumstances, is adequate to produce the phenomena of the *rappings;* but we need not now refer to these. By a curious coincidence, after arriving at the above conclusion respecting the source of the sounds, an instance has fallen under our observation which demonstrates the fact that noises precisely identical with the *spiritual rappings* may be produced in the *knee joint*.

A highly respectable lady, of this city, possesses the ability to develope sounds similar both in character and degree to those professedly elicited by the Rochester impostors from the spiritual world. We have witnessed the production of the sounds by the lady referred to, and have been permitted to examine the mechanism by which they are produced. Without entering, at this time, into a minute anatomical and physiological explanation, it is sufficient to state that, owing to relaxation of the ligaments of the knee joint, by means of muscular action, and pressure of the lower extremity against a point of resistance, the large bone of the leg (the tibia) is moved laterally upon the lower surface of the thigh bone (the femur) giving rise, in fact, to partial lateral dislocation. This is effected by an act of the will, without any obvious movement of the limb, occasioning a loud noise, and the return of the bone to its place is attended by a second sound. Most of the Rochester rappings are also double. It is practicable, however, to produce a single sound, by moving the bone out of place with the requisite quickness and force, and allowing it to slide slowly back, in which case it is noiseless.

The visible vibrations of articles in the room situated near the operator, occur if the limb, or any portion of the body, is in contact with them at the time the sounds are produced. The force of the semi-dislocation of the bone is sufficient to occasion distinct jarring of doors, tables, etc., if in contact. The intensity of the sound may be varied in proportion to the force of the muscular contractions, and this will render the apparent source of the rappings more or less distinct.

We have witnessed the repetitions of experiments in the case just referred to, sufficient to exhibit to us all the phenomena of sounds belonging to the Rochester rappings, and without further explanations at this time, we append our names in testimony of the facts contained in the foregoing hastily penned exposition.

University of Buffalo. { AUSTIN FLINT, M. D.
CHARLES A. LEE, M. D.
C. B. COVENTRY, M. D.

Feb. 17, 1851.

The disclosure announced in the foregoing communication occasioned not a little excitement among those who had become interested in the *knockings*. The correctness of the explanation was not only called in question by these, but was doubted by many who had not hesitated to look upon the matter as a gross deception. The Rochester *ladies* of course stoutly denied the imputation that the sounds proceeded from the joints, or were produced by any agency of theirs, and, the next day, they inserted in the daily papers the following card:—

ROCHESTER KNOCKINGS.

To Drs. Flint, Coventry and Lee:—

Gents:—We observe by a communication in the *Commercial Advertiser*, that you have recently made an examination of a highly respectable lady of this city, by which you have discovered the secret of the "Rochester Impostors." As we do not feel willing to rest under the imputation of being impostors, we are very willing to undergo a proper and decent examination, provided we can select three male and three female friends who shall be present on the occasion.

We can assure the public that there is no one more anxious than ourselves to discover the origin of the mysterious manifestations. If they can be explained on "anatomical" and "physiological" principles, it is due to the world that the investigation be made, and that the "humbug" be exposed. As there seems to be much interest manifested by the public on this subject, we would suggest that as early an investigation as is convenient would be acceptable to the undersigned. ANN L. FISH.
MARGARETTA FOX.

The invitation thus proffered was accepted by those to whom it was addressed, and on the following evening, by appointment, the examination took place. After a short delay, the two Rochester females being seated on a sofa, the knockings commenced, and were continued for some time in loud tones and rapid succession. The "spirits" were then asked "whether they would manifest themselves during the sitting and respond to interrogatories?" A series of *raps* followed, which were interpreted into a reply in the affirmative. The two females were then seated upon two chairs placed near together, their heels resting on cushions, their lower limbs extended, with the toes elevated and the feet separated from each other. The object in this experiment was to secure a position in which the ligaments of the knee joint should be made tense, and no opportunity offered to make pressure with the foot. We were pretty well satisfied that the displacement of the bones requisite for the sounds could not be effected unless a fulcrum were obtained by resting one foot upon the other, or on some resisting body.

The company, seated in a semi-circle, quietly waited for the "*manifestations*" for more than half an hour, but the "spirits," generally so noisy, were now dumb. The position of the younger sister was then changed to a sitting posture, with the lower limbs extended on the sofa, the elder sister sitting in the customary way, at the other extremity of the sofa. The "spirits" did not choose to signify their presence under these circumstances, although frequently requested so to do. The latter experiment went to confirm the belief that the younger sister alone produces the *rappings*. These experiments were continued until the females themselves admitted that it was useless to continue them longer at that time, with any expectation of *manifestations* being made.

In resuming the usual position on the sofa, *knockings* were very soon begun to be heard. It was then suggested that some other experiment be made. This was assented to, notwithstanding the first was, in our minds, amply conclusive. The experiment selected was, that the knees of the two females should be firmly grasped with the hands so applied that any lateral movement of the bones would be perceptible to the touch.

The pressure was made through the dress. It was not expected to prevent the sounds, but to ascertain if they proceeded from the knee joint. It is obvious that this experiment was necessarily far less demonstrative, to an observer, than the first, because if the bones were distinctly felt to move, the only evidence of this fact would be the testimony of those whose hands were in contact with them. The hands were kept in apposition for several minutes at a time, and the experiment repeated frequently, for the course of an hour or more, with negative results: that is to say, there were plenty of *raps* when the knees were not held, and none when the hands were applied save once as the pressure was intentionally somewhat relaxed (Dr. Lee being the holder,) two or three faint, single *raps* were heard, and Dr. Lee immediately averred that the motion of the bone was plainly perceptible to him. The experiment of seizing the knees as quickly as possible when the knockings first commenced, was tried several times, but always with the effect of putting an immediate *quietus* upon the *manifestations*.

The proposition to bandage the knees was then discussed. This experiment was objected to, on the part of the friends of the females, unless we would concede that it should be an exclusive test experiment. We were not prepared with appliances to render the limb immovable, and therefore declined to have it considered such a test. This was the experiment anticipated, and one which, we presume, the females thought would end in their triumph. A bandage applied above and below the patella, admitting of flexion of the limb, will probably not prevent the displacement, as we have but little doubt had been ascertained by the Rochester females before an examination was invited. Should it become necessary to repeat experiments in other places, in furtherance of the explosion of the imposition, we would suggest that the bandage be not relied upon. Plenty of roller, with lateral splints, firmly applied, so as to keep the limbs extended, and render the joints immovable, would doubtless succeed in arresting sounds so far as they involve the knee joint. It will be observed that, in our exposition, we do not claim that this joint is exclusively the source of sounds, and had our experiments, which were first directed to this joint, failed, we should have proceeded to interrogate, experimentally, other articulations. This, however, as the reader will note, seemed quite unnecessary. The conclusion seemed clear that the *Rochester knockings* emanate from the knee joint.

Since the exposition was published, we have heard of several other cases in which movements of the bones entering into other articulations are produced by muscular effort, giving rise to sounds. We have heard of a person who can develope knockings from the ankle, of several who can produce noises with the joints of the toes and fingers, of one who can render loudly audible the shoulder, and another the hip joint. We have also heard of two additional cases in which sounds are produced by the knee-joint. We have not, as yet, had an opportunity to make a personal examination in any of these cases, or to hear the sounds. The exposure of the imposition opens a new and curious field of physiological inquiry, and we would commend the subject to those who have leisure and facilities for prosecuting it. *Articular* as well as *articulated* sounds seem to claim an investigation which they have not heretofore received. Had the facts which the detection of this trick have developed, been contained in anatomical or physiological treatises, the progress of the deception would have been arrested long ere this. Doubtless these facts are not entirely new—they must have been observed in other cases the histories of which have escaped record. That sounds so loud should originate in the way we have ascertained that they are produced, would surprise even the medical listener, and perhaps seem almost incredible. It is readily conceivable how to other than medical listeners, the phenomena should appear, not only inexplicable, but in a high degree mysterious. The remark was made by many after the explanation was published that it required almost as much stretch of the imagination to believe that such sounds could be produced in joints, as that they involved a supernatural agency. The anatomical conformation of the knee joint is evidently most favourable for the production of loud sounds by displacement. The broad articular surfaces offer considerable space for lateral motion, provided the ligaments are sufficiently relaxed, and the requisite motor force is properly applied.—The relative shortness of the outer condyle of the femur favours the outward displacement, and true dislocation in this direction would be likely to occur, were it not for the numerous strong ligaments which render this the strongest articulation in the body. Owing to the great protection afforded by the ligaments against injuries to which, from the position and relations of this joint, it is particularly exposed, dislocations are, in fact, very rare in their occurrence. The displacement occasioning the *knockings* is sufficient to remove the ridge of bone which divides the two articular surfaces of the upper extremity of the tibia, from its situation in the sulcus between the condyles of the femur, and to carry it, more or less, upon the surface of the outer condyle. This movement gives rise to the first sound, and the return of the bone to its place causes the second sound, which, in the *Rochester knockings*, generally follows quickly upon the first. We are unable to explain fully the precise mechanism by which the displacement is effected. In the case of the lady of this city who produces the *spiritual rappings*, the bone slips outward with very slight voluntary effort, and it is not easy, from her own account, or by manual exploration, to determine the particular muscles that are brought to bear upon the joint. In this case the displacement daily occurs, in bending the limb, when no effort is made to produce it, but, under these circumstances, it is not generally attended with much noise. The bone returns to its place directly the muscular effort which has produced the displacement ceases. To develop sound the displacement must take place with a certain quickness and force, and the latter may be graduated, in some measure, at will. A fulcrum of the foot appears also to be requisite as already stated. The lady just referred to is now able to produce the sounds in one knee only. In early life she had this power in both knees. From the number and volume of the sounds produced, it is evident that both the knees of the Rochester rappers now in this city are endowed with sonorous powers. It might be supposed that the frequent repetitions of these displacements would produce after a time irritation and disease within the joint. In the case of the lady of this city they are followed by some soreness, but in early life, when she was in the habit of practising them daily more or less, she experienced no pain, nor any unpleasant consequences, and she was then able to develope louder sounds than she can at present. How rare are instances of that peculiarity in the condition of the joint which admits of the audible phenomena that have given origin to the new science of *spiritual rappings*, we are unable to say.—That they are not common is evident from the fact that the Rochester imposture has eluded detection so long; and that instances of a similar idiosyncrasy do occur, is shown by the fact that several rappers have appeared in different parts of the country. It is a sad commentary on human nature that the latter should prefer to have adopted and carried on the imposition when they discovered their peculiar power, rather than disclose the secret, and thus put a stop to the progress of the deception.—Mrs. P., the lady of this city, to whom we are much indebted for the means of establishing the exposure to the satisfaction of the public, thus deserves honourable mention, and the thanks of the community. A difficulty with some persons who have visited the *Rochester rappers*, in believing the sounds to be articular arises from the idea that the *raps* come from different quarters of the room, at a distance from the place at which the females are stationed. This difficulty involves several explanatory circumstances. In the first place the sounds do not really come from a distance. It may seem that this is so, but it is a delusion, arising from not appreciating correctly some of the laws of acoustics. We do not ordinarily determine the direction from which aural impressions are received, save by the conjoined exercise of other senses. Variations in the supposed distance of the source of sound may be imitated, simply by variations in intensity of sound, provided the source be not obvious to other senses than hearing. Upon these principles the deceptions of the ventriloquist are based. The ventriloquist does not transmit his voice in different directions, and at various distances, as is vulgarly supposed, but he graduates its intensity so as to make it appear more or less remote, concealing at the same time, all external evidences that *he* makes the sounds, and he relies upon directing, by his conversation, the attention of the audience to particular places, for the success of his effort to make it appear that the sounds proceeded from these places. The knee knockings are muffled by the dress, and the slight movements are also thus concealed; hence, females make the best impostors in this line. The *raps* are then conducted by whatever solid substances are in contact with the limb, or body. The *Rochester knockers* prefer that their visitors should be seated around a long table, they sitting at one extremity of the table. Placing the limb, then, in contact with any part of the table, the knockings seem to be upon the latter. But if the limb is in contact only with the floor, the sounds will appear to come from below. The Rochester females, when they wish to give exhibitions of the sounds, sometimes stand near a door. If they touch the door with a limb, or rest against it, the sounds seem to come from the door, and the door may be felt to vibrate. If they stand at a little distance from the door, the sounds appear to come from below. The *raps* do not, in reality, ever appear to come from much distance, unless the delusion is aided by a vivid imagination, or a degree of credulousness very easily operated on. The loudness of the sounds will, aside from the degree of motive power and quickness by which the displacement is effected, depend on the conducting properties of different bodies in contact.

That part of this scheme of imposition which relates to the communications made by means of the *knockings*, opens a field of curious inquiry not devoid of interest and importance. Admitting that the sounds are shown to be physically produced, and dependent upon the volition of those engaged in conducting the deception, some, who have been impressed by the degree of penetration manifested in the accuracy of certain of the responses, and the striking character of the fancied revelations, will ask, "How are these phenomena to be accounted for?" In accounts that have been published by many—we doubt not well-meaning, and on most subjects, sensible persons—there are statements which, to the reader who does not see fit to deny in *toto* the veracity and intelligence of the narrators, certainly must appear extraordinary. We do not propose to discuss at length this view of the subject. To do this does not belong to us, and would be inappropriate in the pages of a medical journal. We will offer but a few remarks.

Having traced the *knockings* to their source, explained the mechanism of their production, and thus divested them of their supernatural character and of all mystery, the field of inquiry just referred to presents an aspect different from that which it had prior to the exposition. While the origin of the sounds was unknown, the belief in their spiritual derivation would be entertained by those whose mental constitution and habits favoured credulity in such matters, and the communications would be received with a corresponding degree of faith; and even some not over-credulous persons might reason themselves into the conviction that the sounds must be due to intelligent, invisible spirits, from the apparent utter impossibility of accounting, by any other hypothesis, for the information thereby obtained. But assuming that the deception is unmasked, and the mode in which it is conducted satisfactorily explained, it follows, of course, that the communications are part and parcel of the humbug, and it only remains to show how it is that they are of a character to occasion surprise and astonishment. This question might be disposed of, so far as the present subject is concerned, by saying that phenomena of the same character and equally extraordinary, occur in connexion with fortune-telling, into which it is not professed that spiritual agencies enter, and which no one supposes to involve aught beyond human sagacity. The question covers all the various modes of imparting pretended supernatural revelations.

Much is due to the laws of probabilities alone—in other words, many of the wonders are coincidences, which always occur in a series of random guesses. This plain fact is not always recollected, viz.: That whenever a response involves either an affirmative or a negative, the chances that it will be right or wrong are exactly equal. Guesses under such circumstances, in the long run, will be as often true as false. It may be admitted, however, that the whole philosophy of the matter is not resolvable into the laws of probabilities; other reasons must therefore be given. Several reasons suggest themselves, some of which we will mention, without attempting to assign to them, respectively, their precise force.

A person of close observation and of great shrewdness can acquire a degree of skill in furnishing communications purporting to be spiritual, which can hardly be appreciated by one who has not given much thought to the subject. This is a kind of acquirement not sought for, except by those who mean to make it subservient to deception; and, therefore, by most persons it is but little understood. Let an individual of proper capacity, make it a business to study the significance of every slight movement, intonation of voice, and expression of countenance, as criteria of concealed thoughts, and let this pursuit be prosecuted for years, under the incentives afforded by the love of gain or applause, and the fear of detection, and the tact thus acquired will be likely to develop results that appear almost incredible, and by the superstitious are regarded as divinations. This is one consideration to which not a little weight belongs.

Another explanatory consideration is as follows: Persons resorting to oracular communications, in proportion as their minds become excited, and full credence secured, can hardly fail to exhibit, in various ways, indications which are so many clues by which a practised observer is led to apprehend facts supposed to be completely hidden. A person who has been much interested in the *knockings*, and who believes that there exists a kind of mesmeric relation between the females and the questioners, by means of which the knowledge of the latter is perceived by the former, informed us that he observed those persons who had full faith that they should obtain true responses generally got them, while those who were incredulous were unsuccessful. We do not doubt the correctness of this observation, and it is fully explained by reference to the consideration just stated.

They, too, who become converts, are anxious to explain any errors and incongruities in the Sibylline responses, and are ready to accept explanations which are only pertinent by a large latitude of construction.—They have an eager desire that what they seek to have communicated shall be communicated, and are ready to adopt any kind of interpretation which will secure the credit of the spirit which condescends to hold intercourse with them. It is sufficiently obvious to those who have made the *art of discovering truth by observation* a subject of study, that a pre-conceived notion often gives a bias even to the exercise of the senses. Not a few of the *false facts* of science are thus derived. Persons are apt to see precisely what they have pre-determined they shall see. How much more is it to be expected that this self-deception will be operative, when, instead of the sober realities of scientific research, the credulous mind is in pursuit of information to be imparted by miraculous means!

Again, the impression produced by successful hits in any of the arts of soothsaying or conjuration, is naturally greater than is consistent with a due regard to the failures. The number of the latter is forgotten, while the former are remembered, and thus acquire an undue preponderance.—More especially this consideration will apply to the prodigies related in written narratives, taking cognizance of those things which are only wonderful when isolated. The principle is the same as that upon which certificates of secret nostrums appeal to the confidence of the public. Admitting the certificates to be authentic, and even true in point of fact, we have only the extraordinary cures, without any of the host of cases in which the effect of the remedy was either nugatory or pernicious. These cases may predominate immensely over those in which benefit was attributed, while the latter, if considered exclusively, seem to furnish an overwhelming mass of evidence. We might add to these considerations, others; but we have already said more upon this branch of the subject than we had intended, and perhaps more than the indulgence of our readers will lead them to excuse. We must offer as an apology for according to the subject so much space, in addition to the reasons before assigned, the personal interest in it growing out of the part we have taken in the detection and disclosure of the source of the Rochester knockings. In engaging in this investigation, we literally followed the scriptural injunction, to "believe not every spirit, but try the spirits." The result is an exposition, the correctness of which rests, in the first place, upon a train of reasoning, which we claim to be in itself conclusive; and, in the second place, upon demonstrative evidence, tested by experiments which may be readily repeated and extended in all places where the *knockings* may be re-produced. It remains to see whether this result will succeed in bringing the career of this singular species of imposture to a close, and thus, to say the least, diverting the current of credulity into some new channel.

Certain physical phenomena in addition to the knockings, are said to be occasionally produced in connexion with the latter; such as moving of tables and chairs; opening and shutting bureau drawers, pulling the hair, etc., of persons assembled to witness the exhibition, and various other palpable demonstrations of what is claimed to be an unknown and mysterious agency. With regard to these phenomena we have only to say that none of them have fallen under our observation, nor are we aware that any have, as yet, been exhibited in this city, although we understand it has been intimated that they will appear by and by. Assuming that such phenomena do take place, we leave for others the task of explaining the mechanism by which they are produced.

So much for that matter. In addition to this, however, I am permitted by a gentleman and his wife, whose names I am at liberty to give to the public, to make the following statement of their detection of a fraud practised in a so called spiritual circle, corroborating the testimony of the medical gentlemen already given. They state that the first circle established in this city was instituted, so far as they know, at their house, and that the developments were therefore made under their own eye, and in their own hearing. I am informed by them that the usual mode of these communications alleged to be spiritual was by sounds, which may be best characterized as "rappings," resembling the noise which may be produced by rapping on a board with the finger-joints. The party would gather around a table, and place their hands upon it, but no one was permitted to look under the table. Presently the sounds would be heard, and the person professing to be a medium would ask questions, to which answers were returned, spelled out by the alphabet. Suppose the so called spirits wished to have a change made in the position of some unbelieving visiter, as happened in the case of a physician of this district, who waited on certain "Rappers" in Arch Street. Let the alphabet be in use, the medium would begin, A, B, C—and at C, there would be three raps. Then begin again, and when H is reached, there will be three raps, and so on at every letter until the word is spelled out. This gentleman, to whom I have referred, tells me that he became suspicious that the mysterious noises were produced by the feet of the operator, and, watching his opportunity, he at last detected the medium in the imposture. His wife made a similar discovery in the case of another circle, corroborating the same truth and exposing the same trick, and they are prepared in the proper form and time, to state with details, which I of course do not wish to mention, more than I should deem it prudent to specify on this occasion. Suffice it to say, without any knowledge of the facts substantiated by the physicians to whose report I have alluded, they arrived at precisely the same conclusion, and indignantly repudiated the whole affair as a miserable trick.

A gentleman who permits me, if I see fit, to use his name, has furnished me with the details of a specimen of the truthfulness of the manifestations of these so called spirits. He inquired whether the spirit of his mother was present? He was told that she was. He next inquired in what year she had died—was it in such or such a year? and was informed in what year she had died. Next, he wished to know *where* she had departed this life? Was it in such, or in such another place? He was told also where she had died. The believers then asked whether the answers were correct? He smiled, and told them there was a slight discrepance between the facts and the spiritual statement, because his mother was still living and in good health in this city. He was unable to get any more answers out of the spirits—they were dumb, and seemed to be sulky, but he was admonished that his course was not a fair one, because wicked spirits sometimes attend these meetings and take a malicious pleasure in giving incorrect answers! And is it possible that sensible people—sane men and women, can be gulled by a subterfuge so silly as this? The wise man tells us, "In vain is the snare spread in the sight of any *bird*," and can persons in their sober senses suffer themselves to be deceived by a fraud so transparent? "*Wicked spirits*," forsooth!

The other day, a gentleman who is something of a wag, was telling, with a sober countenance, a believer in these spiritual manifestations how in the evening he had heard a mysterious noise, coming thump, thump,

thump, down the flight of stairs behind his office in his store on the wharf, produced, as in his heart he well knew, by a venerable rat that was making off with a bone, though this he kept to himself, contenting himself with a statement of the fact, without any explanation; and after hearing the solemn narrative, the believer replied, looking earnestly at him, "*William, thee is a medium.*"*

The answers which are given by many of these "spirits" are usually of the most trivial character, so intrinsically devoid of every attribute which could possibly verify their claim to preternatural agency, that we are at a loss to account for the respect which is paid to them. Either they communicate intelligence which is already known to the querist, and therefore of no practical advantage, or they make "revelations," the truth of which cannot be tested by any means in the compass of human ability. They will tell you, perhaps, the year in which your friend died, by a lucky guess, but why need you go to the spirit world for information you already possess? And certainly it is nothing wonderful that there should, now and then, be a shrewd guess, especially when the question is asked by a credulous believer, who can control neither the expression of his countenance nor the intonations of his voice. The Germans have a proverb, to the purport, *that a blind pig will sometimes find an acorn;* what marvel then, if a trickster should sometimes hit the right answer, in a game of chances, in which the odds are so greatly in his favour?

If these spirits would tell you something of practical benefit, it would be less a matter of wonder, in this utilitarian age that Yankees should have started this spirit notion. If they would tell the brokers what stocks to buy, or the dry goods or flour merchant how to regulate his purchases, there would be some show of reason in the deference paid to them. This was the style in which the spirits of olden time instructed devotees at their shrine. They were accustomed to inquire what would be the success of any given enterprise, and in those days spirits gave very shrewd guesses, and the *medium* did really at times give very remarkable answers, as may be seen by this caution in the book of Deuteronomy, xiii. 1—3: "If there arise among you a prophet, or a dreamer of dreams, and giveth thee a sign or a wonder, and the sign or the wonder come to pass, whereof he spake to thee saying, Let us go after other gods, which thou hast not known, and let us serve them; thou shalt not hearken unto the words of that prophet, or that dreamer of dreams, for the Lord your God proveth you, to know whether ye love the Lord your God with all your heart and with all your soul." This, you will observe, is something different from producing three raps under the leaf of a table, or cracking the knee joints ad libitum.

We will, however, suppose, for the sake of argument, that these sounds are not produced in the manner described in the report of the New York physicians: we can still furnish a clue by which the phenomenon may be explained, without taxing the strength of departed spirits. I am prepared to suggest, for your own satisfaction, an experiment which has been tested by some of my friends, and which will show that the magnetic principle in the human system can affect inert matter in a very singular manner. If some seven or eight persons will lay their hands on a small table, and keep them in that position for half an hour, the table will become magnetized, and it will move and follow the parties just as a needle pursues the magnet.

In certain abnormal conditions of the human body, the system has been

* The friends, as a body, repudiate the Rappers.

known to be surcharged with an electric or magnetic power, which has produced the most surprising results. A case is on record, on the authority of Dr. Emerich, professor of theology at Strasburg, of a young lady whose person was so surcharged with electricity, that she sometimes imparted strong shocks to those standing near her, though the latter frequently did not touch her.

Professor Emerich declares that one day, when he was in another room, she sent him a smart shock, and, when he hastened to her room, she said to him, laughing, "Oh, you felt it, did you?" The lady was an invalid at the time, and her illness terminated fatally. Strange as this may appear, it is a fact, well known to naturalists, that the *gymnotus electricus* possesses a power by which, without any actual contact, it stuns its prey by an electric stroke, and seems, at will, to direct this force with precision. It may, therefore, be that the "rappings" are, in some instances, due to this very cause, and where the knee-joints are not in fault, we should look to this rationale as the next in probability. Other correlative phenomena may be reduced to the same principle, and I am persuaded that the most marvellous of them will ultimately find their solution in the laws which govern the operations of the magnetic fluid. On the supposition, however, that they are even the direct product of a foreign spiritual agency, the doctrines developed and published by the believers in these new revelations are such that no man who would deem the shipwreck of Christian faith a calamity can, for a single moment, give place to them. The design of nine-tenths of these miserable productions is patent upon every page, and the object manifestly is to impair the authority of the Sacred Scriptures, and, by holding forth the Bible—God's precious Book of Truth, as the object of the bitterest scorn and contempt, to destroy the only foundation of comfort in life and death. They would take away the Gospel of Christ and the doctrines of Paul; and, after discarding the voice of revelation, and excluding the light which beams on every page of the sacred volume, what do these spirit philosophers offer in exchange? They take from us the bread of life, and they offer us husks upon which the swine do feed. We do not want their swill. They may carry it to their Fourierites and their Socialists, and offer it to the synagogue that would blot out the word Retribution from the statute books of God and man. They may spread it before the brotherhood that would break up the institution of the family, which is the foundation of all social law, and the basis of all social happiness, and let the clique, who hate the very name of chastity and virtue, batten on the filthy offal, but we will none of it! You would scarcely have patience to listen to the style in which these filthy dreamers foam out their own shame, and I confess I have very little disposition to honour them by a quotation; but a few sentences extracted from one of their books may serve as a brief and yet sufficient example.

"The subject of the authority of the Bible is presented for investigation in this Lecture, not because it is possessed of that intrinsic importance which would demand a laboured argument, but because it has been a subject which is made prominent and conspicuous through the force of human ignorance and bigotry. For long ages in the past, mankind have received the Bible with the most profound and solemn reverence. They have looked upon it as a book which is intrinsically holy, every word and sentence of which are the result of a direct influx from the Divine Mind, and therefore authoritative in the most literal and unlimited sense. So far has this reverence for the Bible extended, that individuals, whose reason and judgment were not sufficiently blinded to receive all its teachings, have been denominated infidels and heretics, and have been treated as the vilest sinners by those whose faith in the writings of this book has rendered them professedly holy. The Bible has thus been made the standard, immovable and fixed, for all thought and action with reference to subjects of morals or religion. This has been regarded as *the* book which God has given to the world as an expression of His will, and as a revelation of the destiny which He has designed for His creatures. In this, it has been supposed, is contained the records of truth which are unmarred and unsullied, by any admixture of earthly error, and have their original source in the great vortex of life and love which exists in the inconceivable depths of space. According to the profound, but bigoted, emotions of the religionist in reference to this book, the minister of the temple has made this a basis for the delivery of lengthy sermons and tedious prayers; and, in compliance with the commands which are here enjoined, the people attend to the external forms of worship, communion, and baptism, as the means of saving their souls from hell. The superstitions which belong to the past have thus been brought into the sphere of the present age, and the mass are willing to be bound and crushed by those burdening chains which have been placed upon the minds and hearts of all past generations."

This book was written by Spirits of the Sixth Circle, R. P. Ambler, medium, and it is inscribed "to all aspiring souls, who seek for truth on earth and freedom in the spheres:" to *them* "this volume is affectionately dedicated by its unseen authors." If any "aspiring soul" adopt the teachings of this book, it will not rise very high, or make any great attainments in knowledge, virtue, or happiness, either in this life, or in that which is to come. Apart from the wickedness of holding any communication with circles favouring this foul blasphemy in their creed, and worshipping, as they most undoubtedly do, in their hymns and invocations, the spirits with whom they wish to converse, what parent, husband, brother, or child—what man or woman to whom that word "home" is precious above all the treasures of earth—can look with indifference upon this infernal effort to break down the barriers of society, and erect upon the ruins of our domestic altars the filthy shrines of unbridled licentiousness and profligacy? This is the ultimate tendency of the whole movement. Good men may be, and good men have been, decoyed into the meshes of this net; but we have confidence in the power of the grace and truth of the God of the Bible, that this aggressive movement upon the bulwarks of revealed truth will share the fate of every similar weapon formed against Zion. It will not only recoil and be broken, but its point will turn and pierce the hand that hurls it against the breastplate of the Prince of Truth.

www.ingramcontent.com/pod-product-compliance
Lightning Source LLC
LaVergne TN
LVHW011133110826
845150LV00008B/2324
* 9 7 8 1 4 1 8 1 9 4 0 8 6 *